Social Media Marketing 2019

Secret Strategies to Become an Influencer of Millions on Instagram, YouTube, Twitter, and Facebook and Advertise Yourself and Your Personal Brand

Written by Dave Welch

The following eBook is reproduced below with the goal of providing information that is as accurate and reliable as possible. Regardless, purchasing this eBook can be seen as consent to the fact that both the publisher and the author of this book are in no way experts on the topics discussed within and that any recommendations or suggestions that are made herein are for entertainment purposes only. Professionals should be consulted as needed prior to undertaking any of the action endorsed herein.

This declaration is deemed fair and valid by both the American Bar Association and the Committee of Publishers Association and is legally binding throughout the United States.

Furthermore, the transmission, duplication or reproduction of any of the following work including specific information will be considered an illegal act irrespective of if it is done electronically or in print. This extends to creating a secondary or tertiary copy of the work or a recorded copy and is only allowed with an expressed written consent from the Publisher. All additional rights reserved.

The information in the following pages is broadly considered to be a truthful and accurate account of facts and as such any inattention, use or misuse of the information in question by the reader will render any resulting actions solely under their purview. There are no scenarios in which the publisher or the original author of this work can be in any fashion deemed liable for any hardship or damages that may befall them after undertaking information described herein.

Additionally, the information in the following pages is intended only for informational purposes and should thus be thought of as universal. As befitting its nature, it is presented without assurance regarding its prolonged validity or interim quality. Trademarks that are mentioned are done without written consent and can in no way be considered an endorsement from the trademark holder.

Table of Contents

Introduction

Congratulations on downloading *Social Media Marketing 2019!*

This book is optimized for anyone who is looking to discover what trends and marketing strategies are going to be best for 2019. Within this book, we will explore information that is essential for both start-up companies who are just beginning their businesses within 2019, to those who are already in business but looking to maximize their exposure and stay trendy in 2019.

In 2019, the primary focus on all social media platforms is going to be on the social aspect. As businesses have begun to find their way online, all of the soulless, spammy, and generic marketing strategies are dying out. They are quickly realizing that audiences do not respond well to hard pitches or ones that lack any personality to them. Instead, businesses and marketing experts are beginning to recognize that despite most people preferring to shop online these days, they still want a personalized experience that is rich with service and a strong social aspect.

Hearing the call, social media platforms are beginning to rise up to include more features that allow this social, personalized aspect. This is a great way for their users to engage, but it also a powerful marketing tool for businesses wanting to create relationships with their customers. Live videos, stories, video marketing tools, and more are all being included to support brands and customers in having a more personalized connection with each other. Furthermore, algorithms are actually changing to give preference to those who are being social and are in turn hiding those who are not actively engaging with their audience and creating a fun social experience.

In this book, we are going to discover what these different organic and paid marketing strategies are and how they will look going into 2019. You will learn many strategies to take advantage of these features and create success in your business in 2019 by putting the social in social media. If you follow these strategies for Facebook, Instagram, YouTube, and Twitter, your business will be sure to flourish on social media in the coming year.

Chapter 1:
The Importance of Social Media

It is no secret that social media has had a massive impact on businesses over the past five to ten years. As social media continues to grow in popularity, we are seeing more and more of what can arise from this powerful tool. That being said, going into 2019 social media is going to be more important than ever as we project that the power of it will continue to grow bigger and bigger.

At one time, businesses could easily get away with having a small or virtually non-existent web presence. However, as social media begins to grow even more rapidly than ever before, having a non-existent, small, or under qualified social media presence can have a seriously detrimental impact on your business. These days, if your customers cannot reach you on social media, they will likely forget about you. One of the first questions people ask, even in brick and mortar stores, when they are interested in the products is: "are you on social media?"

The way people shop is now heavily influenced by social media. It no longer matters if you are selling products or services online or offline, having a social media presence will be the first thing people look to before purchasing from you. Your social media presence, the way you use social media, and how you build your brand through it will heavily influence whether or not people will shop through your company or if they will choose someone else who has the online presence and impact that they are looking for.

How Social Media Influences Recognition

The first and foremost way that social media will impact your business is by making your brand recognizable to your ideal client. If you leverage your online presence properly, people who come across you will find you memorable. As a result, when they see your brand elsewhere: such as somewhere in their social circle or in person, they will remember who you are. This results in this person feeling far more comfortable with your brand, thus increasing sales.

Building brand awareness on social media offers many unique benefits to you as the brand. For example, you can show your audience many different facets of your brand because they have the capacity to see many different types of content from you. This can range from showing your audience behind-the-scenes information and images that they otherwise would not have seen to showing them up close and personal images of new stock or services being offered so that they can get a first-hand view on what to expect from your new products or services.

If you are looking at social media as a way to build brand awareness, you need to make sure that you follow the appropriate guidelines to create a brand that cultivates relationships. Adding depth to your image, engaging with your audience, and fostering great customer relationships online all support you in having better recognition. You will learn more about how to create this for Facebook, Instagram, YouTube and Twitter in this very guide.

How Social Media Influences Sales

Social media has been influencing sales for years now. In more recent years, these sales have been directly encouraged by influencers themselves. Individuals who test out your product or service and recommend it directly to their audience are often the ones to thank for many of the sales that come in through your online sales channels. Furthermore, having a strong presence yourself can turn your own brand into an "influencer" brand, thus increasing sales as well. The more people talk about how great your brand is, the further your reach becomes and the more interested people are in your products because you now have what is called "social proof" or evidence that your products or services are as good as you claim them to be. In other words, these are like having a great testament or review that supports you in earning greater sales numbers.

In the online space, your target audience gets the opportunity to openly see how you interact with individuals who support you. They can learn all about you by seeing what you post about, what your captions are about, and how (or if) you comment back to those who are showing support on your profile. This means that you have a great opportunity to give first-hand insight as to how you treat those who support your business. Here, you can display how effective, efficient, and kind your customer support team is, you can show how much you appreciate your loyal customers, and you can give new customers a wonderful opportunity to see the greatness in your brand and choose to purchase through you. It is a powerful way to add many dimensional layers to your sales process. These are great for helping to remove the "pushy salesman" image from customers' minds (you know the ones: they stalk you around brick-and-mortar shops to try and push you to help them reach their quotas,) and introduce them to a new, more compassionate and considerate form of sales.

How Social Media Benefits Your Business Directly

Your business and bottom line also stand to earn many great benefits from social media. Aside from the obvious, more customers, using social media can save you a lot of money. Cheaper advertising, free exposure, and a new sales channel all add to the reasons why social media will have a huge impact on supporting you in running your business. For those looking to gain more exposure for half the cost (or less,) or those looking to add a new sales channel to their business, having a social media presence will be life-changing. Greater sales with less overhead are always good news for business owners.

I'm willing to bet that if you are reading this book, you already have a good idea as to the very fact that social media itself is extremely important. Incorporating an online channel for your business may not have made a lot of sense in the past, but nowadays it makes absolutely no sense not to. Even if you are a brick-and-mortar business that appears to have no need for an online presence, such as a dentist or a law firm, having an online presence will change your business. Getting this exposure is crucial to any business that wants to remain afloat in coming years. This was already growing in truth in the past, but it has become an absolute at this point.

Chapter 2:
How Social Media Will Impact Your Business in 2019

Social media has seen many changes in how it benefits and impacts companies in the past decade. From being a platform that was mostly concerned in peer to peer connections to becoming highly popular for businesses to become acquainted with customers, social media has definitely changed in what it's focus is. Nowadays, most social media platforms actually feature many business-specific settings and features that support you in creating and building your online presence. These settings are rapidly growing and evolving, but they ultimate aim toward fulfilling one specific goal: creating intimate and genuine connections between businesses and new and existing customers.

In 2019, there are many projected trends that are going to impact how businesses communicate with their customers in the online space. Understanding and following these trends will ensure that you remain relevant and visible to your target audience. If you are just starting out, these will be necessary for you to quickly become noticed without instantly falling to the bottom of the pile and getting lost in it all. If you have a presence already, adjusting to accommodate for these trends and watching as they integrate and grow further is important as they will keep you relevant and help you continue growing in 2019.

Mainstream Influencer Potential

One phenomenal benefit that businesses stand to gain is having their businesses seen and shared by mainstream influencers. More and more influencers continue to arise on the scene, many of which are making it their primary purpose to become well-known by the various target audience.

Amongst those influencers will include individuals who are targeting *your* audience. Because this particular career of choice is growing massively, you have a growing capacity to get in front of your target audience through the influence of their favorite influencers.

As a brand seeking to launch or grow in 2019, accessing the support of influencers means that you have the capacity to reach your target audience infinitely faster. They are like the marketing masters of the modern generation. As their audience grows, you have the capacity to reach an even larger audience through them. Fortunately, working together with influencers is not nearly as hard (or expensive) as working together with an advertising agency. This means that you get maximum exposure while spending far less on your business. This is particularly great for smaller businesses who are coming up on the scene as influencer agreements are generally affordable to even the newest and smallest of budding businesses and entrepreneurs.

Video Advertisements

Video content is massively growing in popularity. With virtually every platform nurturing video content in exceedingly more prominent ways, you now have the opportunity to appeal to your audience by not just showing them pictures of your products or services, but by giving them a real-life video example. This means you can easily film a video of you introducing new products or services and share that video with your audience. Or, better yet, many platforms now have a LIVE video feature which enables you to share real-time. This means that you can share your product in front of live viewers who are able to then ask questions and feel a more personalized experience from it all. This enables you to create a sense of realism for them, making your brand and product far more desirable and approachable by your target audience.

When it comes to video advertisements, there are many free and paid options that you can take advantage of across virtually all of the most popular platforms. It is your choice as to whether you want to do an organic video share where you do not pay for anything but encourage your audience to share so the video reaches more people, or if you want to pay a fee and have your video pushed in front of more viewers by the algorithms of whichever platform you are using. This means that you can take advantage of one of the best marketing strategies to date with or without spending any money to do so.

Virtual and Augmented Reality Filters

One especially fascinating thing that is being rolled out on a bigger scale in 2019 is having virtual and augmented reality filters made more mainstream for businesses to use. Phones are being created with these features built-in and social media platforms are projected to be taking advantage of these features by offering users way to create their own virtual and augmented reality filters that can be shared across their platforms. As a business, this means that you will have a new and even more interactive way of enabling your customers to see and experience your products before choosing to purchase them.

Another way that brands can begin incorporating these features into their companies is by creating custom filters or emojis that can be designed by their audience. This means that as a user can upload their face through a specialized camera and take advantage of your filter or customization option to create their own custom emoticon. Although features like this do not necessarily result in direct product sales, they do make for a wonderful way to maximize your exposure in a fun and relevant way. As a result, more people are likely to recognize your brand and thus you are discovered by more potential customers.

Specific Targeting Opportunities

As social media companies continue to grow their platforms to incorporate businesses, their advertising features are becoming even more high tech than ever before. This means that going into 2019 you can expect to see all of the most popular social media platforms roll out even more features that will support you in targeting your audience more efficiently and reaching them more directly. As a result, any funds you invest into your paid advertising features will be spent more efficiently and will result in you having greater conversions from your paid advertising campaigns.

Combining your paid campaigns with other popular features such as the virtual and augmented reality filters or video advertisements will work together to create extremely powerful marketing strategies for companies of any size. Because of how easy it is to get into the same stream of marketing as mainstream companies are, it is becoming increasingly more efficient for new and small businesses to reach their audience with the same impact that large companies have been doing for years. As a person in business in 2019, this means that you are seeing your opportunity of doing successful business increasing exponentially, bringing you into a similar playing field as all of the larger companies and corporations on the scene.

Chapter 3:
Where Do You Need to Spend Time?

Determining which social media platform your business should be on requires some attention, intention, and consideration. You want to make sure that every effort is focused on something that is likely to actually turn results for you. For this reason, choosing the proper platforms is important. There are many ways that you can determine which platforms you should be spending the most of your time on. These ways typically require you to consider which platform caters specifically to your target audience, what it is that you are trying to sell or share, how, and why.

In this chapter, we are going to discover how you can choose which of the four platforms discussed in this book will be best for you. You will discover whether you should be spending most of your time on Facebook, Instagram, YouTube, Twitter, or a mixture of a few or all of these platforms to get the best exposure for your business. You will also discover which of these may be least effective for your business if there is one. That way, you can determine where the best places to focus your effort are and how you can maximize your attention there to increase your exposure and thus increase your bottom line.

Who is Facebook For?

Facebook is a platform that should be used by virtually everyone. Having some form of presence on Facebook is important as this is one of the first places people are going to look to see if you exist in the online space. *All* businesses are on Facebook, so if you are not there is no way anyone is likely to find you. If you are on Facebook, however, and your target audience does not spend a lot of time on Facebook, this does not necessarily mean that you need to spend all of your time on

Facebook. Instead, you can nurture this one a bit less than others while still keeping it relevant enough that people can find it if they search for you.

Facebook has more than 1.44 billion active users each month, which is a massive audience for any business to get in front of. Because of the sheer size of this platform, businesses can guarantee that their audience is spending time here at least a few times per week, but generally a few times per day. The audience on Facebook varies massively between generations and ages, and their interests and regular activities. The most active age group on Facebook, however, ranges between 25-34 years old. If your target audience lies within this age range you should be spending a greater amount of time on Facebook. If your audience is between the ages of 18-55 Facebook is still a great platform to be on, though engagement and interaction will likely be lower for you.

Another great thing about Facebook is their analytics. When you are on Facebook as a business you gain great insight into the analytics of who is following you, what their demographics are, and to what degree they are engaged with you. This means that you can gain clarity on who your target audience is to an even more specific degree. As a small business, the amount of information you can gain from Facebook analytics alone is highly valuable. You can use this information to support you in having more clarity when developing your ad campaigns, as well as when inputting information into paid advertising platforms to ensure that you reach your target audience as directly as possible. This information can be used both on Facebook itself and on any other platform you may desire to advertise on. actively engaging with posts and sharing information with their friends. This means this is the perfect platform for you to have an engaged following.

Who is Instagram For?

Instagram is an extremely popular platform for anyone who is running a business that caters to those who fall between the ages of 18-29 years old. Instagram is an application where many turn to for visual inspiration, making it a great platform to market on. If you are running a business that sells products or services that can be exposed and shared through visual aspects (which accounts for most businesses,) Instagram would be a great platform for you to spend time on.

With Instagram, it is important to understand that if your demographic is older, such as 35-40+ years old, there is a good chance that you will not connect with them very well on Instagram. For that reason, if you are catering to an older demographic you may wish to skip over this platform entirely.

Who is Twitter For?

Twitter is a platform that is used mostly by those between the ages of 18-55. It is really popular amongst those who are interested in the news such as politics or current events, though you often see younger users on there as a way to stay up to date with their favorite brands and idols. Using Twitter is a great way to access a large market, though it does have a learning curve involved that may be more challenging than other platforms. That being said, this book is the perfect place to go to master Twitter, so if you want to take advantage of this platform you are in the right place!

Like Facebook, Twitter has a healthily dispersed platform that ranges in age, demographic, and interests. This means that virtually everyone can benefit from Twitter. Another great aspect of Twitter is that you can see what everyone is saying about you by simply typing your name in the search bar at the top of the application or webpage. As a result, you can easily engage with everyone who even mentions your brand's name, maximizing your exposure in an extremely simple way.

Who is YouTube For?

YouTube is another great platform to be on and, when used right, can be leveraged by most companies. Video marketing does take more effort than other platforms, so it is generally recommended to start using it after you have already built some level of a following online. That being said, the sooner you can get into this marketing strategy the better since video marketing is projected to grow much larger and more rapidly in 2019.

With YouTube, you can easily educate your audience about your products and services. Sharing information, advice, tips, early insights, sneak peeks, and other great content with them online is the perfect way to start leveraging your business online. You can also work toward making a video that can go viral by making something that is funny and relatable or extremely interesting and educational to share with your audience. If the video is short enough and powerful enough you can easily grow it far beyond your basic audience and get your company in front of the eyes of many new prospective clients. If you have the right equipment and are ready to begin making professional-level films, YouTube can be a great place to spend time. However, if you do not and you are not yet ready to film professional-level films, it would be best to wait. The standards on video marketing amongst most audiences these days are quite high, so anyone who is not yet ready to directly compete with the high quality of others in their niche should avoid this until they are ready.

Chapter 4
Why Use Facebook in 2019

Facebook has been around for about a decade and the way it has been used for business has rapidly changed over the years. Heading into 2019, Facebook is an essential tool for people to use if they want to be discovered by any potential customers. Facebook will be essential in helping you locate both local and long-distance clients. The realization that Facebook for business is important has been increasingly apparent over the past few years, but in 2019 it will no longer be a question. Instead, it will be a no-brainer. Either you enter the Facebook world and you increase visibility and exposure, or you rapidly lose traction to those who are willing to.

Going into 2019, many of the trends that we have seen becoming popular in 2018 will become even more popular in 2019. There will also be many more that rise in popularity as the trends that are already on the uptrend evolve for greater use. Some of these include things like:

- Automated marketing (i.e. chatbots, customer profiling)
- Video marketing (i.e. sharing YouTube videos, native videos, live videos)
- Integration (i.e. being integrated into third-party apps for greater usages)
- Social CEOs (such as Mark Zuckerberg himself)
- Analytic Monitoring (for greater accuracy with ads)

The diversity of how social media integrates with people's lives and the many ways that it is being used is going to have a major impact on your business in 2019. These days, virtually everything is tied in with social media in some way. For your business, this means that as social media developers continue to evolve this integration, you continue to have greater access at having the opportunity to integrate directly with many different highly-engaged and interactive parts of your consumer's days.

Facebook tends to be at the forefront of these evolutions due to it being the leading social media platform. Facebook also owns Instagram meaning that anything you see rolling out on Facebook will inevitably be adjusted and rolled out on Instagram in the coming weeks or months.

Using Facebook is ultimately the best way to ensure that you are reaching your audience in the best capacity. Facebook will integrate with many other social media and non-social media sites, such as Pinterest, blogs, various membership accounts, and even e-mail and other similar sites. Being available on these sites ensures that no matter where your audience is logging in, they are able to access your business in some capacity. Furthermore, it means that when they *do* log in, it goes into tracking for analytics and makes your own advertising capacity even more accurate.

Getting started on Facebook now, or developing your Facebook presence further in 2019 will ensure that as these trends continue to strengthen and increase that you remain at the forefront. As social media takes off, you can guarantee that the bigger your presence is the more you will benefit. Therefore, maximizing your audience right now will guarantee your continued growth and exposure over the coming year, and for many years to come. It is a no-brainer: if you are running a business in 2019, you need to be running an online presence through Facebook in 2019 and nurturing it regularly.

Problems to Avoid

One thing many people tend to run into troubles with on Facebook is feeling as though they have wasted their time and funds. This is often a problem people face because they do not take the time to understand the platform and utilize it effectively. With minimal understanding of the algorithm, it can be easy to become lost in the sea of all of the others posting on the platform. Creating a strong page, building a community, maximizing customer relationships, and working toward creating a strong organic reach before moving into paid advertising is important with Facebook. These activities will ensure that you know exactly who your target audience is and how you can approach and reach them through your organic reach as well as your paid reach without feeling as though you have wasted your time or funds.

Another thing that can happen on Facebook pages is that people do not feel as though they are a part of a community. Instead, it can feel like they are just reading a magazine that has been curated for them. To bypass this, you can use Facebook groups as a way to build a community and have engaged interaction between your business and your audience. By spending the time genuinely building the community through the efforts that you will learn about in chapters 5 and 6, you will discover how you can overcome this "faceless, soulless CEO" symptom and create a powerful image that people are eager to interact with, follow, and listen to.

Chapter 5:
Organic Facebook Marketing

One of the best aspects of being able to market on social media lies in being able to market both for free and paid. While paid advertising generally offers the capacity to create a wider reach quicker, free advertising brings what is called "organic reach," meaning exposure that is not paid for. Typically, social media loves to see pages that have organic reach as this shows that your audience is naturally attracted to you and your products or services. This means that you are more likely to be shown in the newsfeed and that your paid advertisements will have a greater reach as well because you are seen as popular and likable, therefore the Facebook algorithm will favor your content over the content of others who are struggling to create an organic impact.

Free marketing through Facebook comes in many different forms. These different forms should each be used efficiently to create a more dynamic image, thus intensifying the level of interest people have in you. While in the past merely sharing images was plenty enough to get your name out there, these days your audience wants more. They want to know your brand and the faces that represent your brand, as well as the unique quirks about you. Your followers want the inside scoop on who you are, what you care about, and what this means for them. They also want this to be incorporated into your brand as it adds to the many layers of intimacy shared between the social CEO and their audience. In other words, your followers are tired of faceless, soulless corporations that are led by people they never see, hear, or engage with. They want to know the person running the brand, and they want to know the brand. The more you spend time getting your brand's identity and your own (parts) of your identity out there, the better. Not only is this the purpose of social media itself, but it is also an extremely important way of creating a relationship with your followers and customers and building intensity and momentum in 2019 in the Facebook world.

The following portion of this chapter is going to be devoted to showing you the many ways that you can use free Facebook features to begin building the dynamic and texturized image of your brand and the faces that represent it. This way, you can begin creating powerful and meaningful relationships with your audience that will actually support *both* of you in supporting the other. So, your outreach supports your client by enabling you to understand them and provide better products and services, just as their reciprocation of your outreach provides you with increased sales numbers.

Building and Optimizing Your Facebook Page

The first step in being able to have a strong outreach for your audience is having an optimized Facebook page! If you do not yet have a page, this section will walk you through the process of creating one that will be optimal for marketing in 2019. If you do already have a Facebook page, this section will support you in optimizing that page so you can stay relevant and maximize your impact in 2019!

Building your Facebook page consists of many layers in the modern age. At one time, you named the page, added a picture, and began posting. Nowadays, businesses can share images both as profile pictures and cover images, upload stories about how their business was founded, introduce their company and their team members, and so much more. With so many different aspects of your page that can be nurtured, it is important to make sure that you are aware of each component and how it works. This way you can take advantage of all of the many different layers and give your audience plenty of information to get to know you and your brand even more. Which, as you know, is extremely important! The more content your audience can consume about you, the more connected they feel to you and your brand. Therefore, the greater your relationship is from the get-go and the greater your impact is on serving them and maximizing your sales through your Facebook efforts.

Creating A Page

The first thing that you need to do is actually create your page. You will need to be logged in from your personal account to get started. Then, in the sidebar menu where you can locate many different browsing options, discover the option that says "Create a Page." Upon selecting this option you will be given the opportunity to choose from many different business types. You will want to pick the one that best represents your business. If you feel that your brand identifies under many different categories, you will want to choose the one that your audience would be most likely to identify you with.

Once you have chosen the category that your business falls under, you will want to include any further information regarding your business. This includes the name of your business, contact information, and your location (if you have one.) You will also need to pick a name for your page. Picking your name should be simple: you want to choose the name of your business to be the name of your page. This is what people are going to recognize you as; therefore, you want to keep it simple. The easier it is to identify you, the better it will be for your audience when it comes to locating you and learning more about your business.

After you have inputted all of this basic information you can tap "Get Started." This means that your page will officially be created. This also means that you are accepting the terms and conditions for Facebook's Business Pages. For that reason, you may want to take a look at them before tapping "Get Started" just to see what falls within them.

Add Your Pictures

Upon having your page officially created, the first thing that you need to customize is your profile picture and your cover image. Having a clean, professional image in each spot is the best way to keep your page attractive, identifiable, and likely to be engaged with. Many businesses like using their logo as their profile picture. This is a great way to help your audience identify with you, as well as to increase the exposure of your logo so that your audience begins to recognize it as being yours. If you do not have a logo, or you would rather your own image become more recognizable, you can always upload a professional headshot image that accurately reflects your business image. So, for example, if you are a realtor you could use your professional headshot with you in your suit or other work attire as your profile image for your business. Alternatively, if you do have a logo but you would rather use something more personal, you could use your headshot with the logo edited into the bottom left or right corner of the image. Keeping this image clear, professional, and easily identifiable will make it easier for your audience to decide whether or not they want to look at your page. If the image is unclear, confusing, or poor quality, the likelihood of them venturing onto your page is significantly reduced.

For your cover image, the same standards apply. The image should be professional, clean, and clear. You also need to make sure that it is created with the right standards and uploaded on a computer. Uploading the image on your mobile phone can result in it becoming blurry and losing quality, which dampens the competitiveness and attractiveness of your page. When creating this image, make sure that it is at least 400 pixels wide and 150 pixels tall. Your cover image should be something relevant to your business. For example, if you run a grocery store you could include an image of produce here.

If you are not particularly certain about what you want these images to be or you are struggling to create effective ones, you might consider having a professional branding package created for your Facebook page. There are many graphic designers who offer packages as such that will take your logo and create a professional profile and cover images for your page. Some will also create a Canva template or other template in a common image editing software so that you can easily make your own quoted images for your page. Having these professionally made can save you time and give you a more put-together look if you are not confident in your own ability to create a professional and attractive looking image collection for your page. Fiverr and Upwork are great places to look to hire such graphic designers for inexpensive.

Add A Description

Now that your page is created and has its images completed, you need to create your page description! By going to your "About" page you can locate a button that says "Add a Short Description." There, you can add in a short blurb about what your business is all about. You only get 150 characters for this description, so make sure it is clear and concise. For example, for Al's Pancake World you could upload a description that says "Serving the best pancakes in all of America" or for Nancy's Nail Salon you could put "Creative, classy, and unique nail designs for any occasion" or "Specializing in creating unique nail art for the eccentric soul." Keeping the description descriptive yet attractive and intriguing is important as this can help draw people in while also giving them a clear understanding of what you do.

Create A Username

Recently, Facebook introduced usernames for pages. These are shown as "@username" beneath the page name. The purpose of this username is to make it extremely simple for your followers to identify you across multiple platforms. That being said, this username should be one that you can claim across all social media platforms that you intend to use. Make sure you claim it on all and keep it exactly the same so that you are easy to identify. That way, when your followers see your username they can input the exact same username into any other social media website and locate you if you are spending time on it. Your username will also be added at the end of Facebook's URL to provide a direct link to your page on Facebook. They call this a "vanity URL." This vanity URL looks like this when done: *"Facebook.com/username"* making it easy to link to business cards or anywhere else without having a long URL filled with numbers, letters, and varying characters.

You can create your username by clicking "Create a Username for Your Page" in the "Page Settings" section. Once there, choose the username that you want to use and input it. You can use any unused username up to 50 characters in length. Again, make sure that it is clear and concise. Furthermore, just because you have 50 characters does not mean that you need to use them: refrain from adding any unnecessary characters that might make it more of a challenge to remember your username.

Complete the "About" Section

Next, you want to go to the "About" tab on your page and tap "Edit." Here, you can fill in many different pieces of information about your business. You will find the opportunity to input and adjust your business hours, the hours that your customer service reps are available to answer Facebook messages, details about your business, the date it was founded, the type of business it is, and any other links you may want to include, such as a link to your website.

On your About page you will also see a spot called "Story." Here, you can edit your story and include all of the information you desire about how your business came to be, why, and what your mission is within your company. While this is not necessary, having this story fulfilled gives your inspired followers the opportunity to read more about who you are, feel even more connected with your brand, and strengthen that relationship.

Lastly, you can also add team members. Team members can have varying degrees of involvement on the page ranging from being able to monitor comments and delete or respond to them on behalf of the page to being able to completely edit the page and act on behalf of it altogether. Make sure you are mindful of what roles you are giving to each team member to avoid giving too much power to a member you may not want to give it to.

Edit Your Tabs

The last part of customizing your page is editing your tabs. Your tabs are the various "options" people can click to on your page. The ones that Facebook offers include Posts, About, Groups, Community, Videos, Photos, Reviews, Info and Ads, Events, Jobs, Live Videos, Notes, Offers, Services, and Shop. To edit these, simply go to the "Edit Page" setting and choose which tabs you do and do not want to be linked to your page. Those that are will be visible to your audience, offering them the opportunity to browse what lies within them. You can also drag them around to adjust them, placing them in any order you desire. Any that you exclude from the list will not be visible to your audience. Some of these may be irrelevant to your business so hiding these tabs can make it easier for your audience to locate exactly what they need. You can also find "Page Templates" in this section that will automatically choose which tabs are best for your business and organize them in a way that is easy for your audience to navigate to locate the information they want or need.

One tab that you should always keep available no matter what your business type is would be the "Reviews" tab. Some businesses may be eager to hide this tab, particularly if they are new and have no existing reviews. However, this can seem suspicious to your audience as they are often looking for positive reviews to support them in making purchases from you. Having the reviews tab option open and then doing your best to offer amazing products or services and the best customer service can support you in receiving great reviews that will then translate into you having increased sales through your business. Many people do look to Facebook for reviews and may skip over your business in favor of one that is rated well, so be sure not to skip over this or accidentally eliminate it from your page.

Make Your First Post

Now that your page is all customized, it is time to make your first post! To do this, simply go to the "posts" tab and tap where it says "Write a post..." You can post about anything you desire, from welcoming people to your new page or informing them about the current goings on in your business. In the next section of this chapter, "Posting On Your Facebook Page," we will discuss the various types of Facebook posts that exist and how you can use them to amplify your page, ramp up engagement, and gain greater exposure.

Posting On Your Facebook Page

There are several different types of posts that you can make on Facebook to begin building organic audience reach through your page. Ideally, you should be posting three times per day, changing up what style of post that you are sharing each time. As you continue posting and interacting with your audience, you will likely discover that certain posts gain better traction than others. As these types of trends in engagement and response show themselves through your analytics, make sure to follow them as these will support you in staying relevant and getting the best content to your audience. Furthermore, these trends in analytics are often where new marketing trends are born from. Who knows: with the right attention and creativity, you may just find yourself leading the next greatest trend in social media marketing!

The types of posts that you can do on your Facebook page include :

- Status Update
- Link Sharing
- Photos and Videos
- Tagging Products
- Advertising Your Business

- Publishing a Job Post
- Offers and Discounts
- Lists
- Notes
- Milestones
- Events
- Polls
- Q&As
- Shared from Other Sites or Pages

Each of these different post formats are offered directly on your Facebook page when you tap "Post" except for link sharing and shared from other sites or pages. These two are simply a style of post that you create by adding a link or by tapping "share" on someone else's post and sharing it to your business page.

Using these different types of posts allows you to create different styles of posts that are interactive and engaging for your audience. The ones that you should be using most often include sharing photos and videos, status updates, and sharing links or sharing from other pages or sites. The others can be used for specific purposes. For example, if you are looking to introduce a new product or service you can use the polls or Q&A feature. If you and your business are celebrating a milestone, such as a business anniversary, moving into a new location, or launching a new segment of your business, you could use the milestone feature to mark that occasion and celebrate it with your audience.

There are many different creative ways to share these different features with your audience. Using them regularly and using a variety of different ways of sharing means that you are giving your audience the best opportunity to have a unique and interactive experience with your brand. Take advantage of them and, if you are ever uncertain, get creative. Do not be afraid to try new things, step outside of the box, and share in new ways. You may just find that your audience responds in surprising and exciting ways!

Live Videos

Live videos are a more recent and powerful form of sharing with your audience. With live video, you can share real-time with your audience. This means that you can show them new products or services up close and personal, you can do a personalized sharing of information or education with your audience, and you can otherwise engage in powerful video marketing with a highly personalized touch. Using live video makes it feel like your audience is right there with you, deepening your relationship with them and adding a highly personalized element to your Facebook marketing strategy. This live video can also be saved and added to your story feed, meaning anyone who views your Facebook stories can see this live video through your stories. If you save it and publish it on your page, it can also be viewed there, as well as shared. When you do a live video, make sure you share it to your group as well so that your audience has a greater chance of seeing it. This will also support you in promoting your page to your audience who may not be following it yet.

Facebook Stories

Facebook stories feature is an incredible feature that allows you to take short video clips or images and share them into a 24-hour story feed. This feed allows you to share "behind-the-scenes" images and clips of your business with your audience. Stories work much like Snapchat but are built-in to Facebook making them easier to access. You can use fun filters, stickers, and overlays to further customize these images and share them with your audience.

The best way to use stories to market your business is to give exclusive, you-can't-find-this-anywhere-else type images and clips with your audience. If you run a personal brand, share images of your day that relate to your business or share clips of you chatting about the process of creating your next service or product. You can also share information about how much you love your business, how your business ties in with your life, and other tidbits that help your audience feel connected to you. If you run a larger business with employees and a separate brand-entity, you can have the key players in your business sharing images to the stories. Maybe you could share images of your employees at work, have them do little video clips of their daily work activities in a unique way, or even use this as a way to introduce your audience to your employees. Some companies have even granted story-access to their employees and alternated who got to be in control over the stories on a day to day basis so that their audience can get a diversified view of the many people who are behind-the-scenes with the brands they love. Getting creative and sharing personalized content here is a great way to connect with your community and increase brand awareness, relationships, and customer loyalty and interest.

Creating Groups to Build Your Community

Facebook groups are a phenomenal way to begin building a community for your brand. When used properly, Facebook groups can provide your audience with a place to come together and share topics that are relating to your brand. Many companies create these with the intention of interacting with their audience and encouraging their audience to interact together, as well. This is a great way to not only build brand loyalty and create a more personalized presence for your audience but also to see your audience in action. When your audience begins communicating and sharing with each other organically, it becomes easier for you to see what they tend to talk about, what they are interested in, and how they behave. This offers a great opportunity for some market research!

Groups can be made for any variety of reasons. Typically, the group is designed to offer some form of exclusive, members-only benefits that are gained from the person or brand leading the group. So, say you are a life coach, you might create a group intended to support people in leading a more positive lifestyle. Through this intention, you can offer unique incentives to join the group. Then, from within your group, people gain the opportunity to get to know you better. Just like you are getting to know them on a better level and are paying attention to their interests and behavior, your audience will be doing the same with you. They will want to pay attention and see how kind you are, what your personality is like, and how you offer support to your audience. This can be on a personal basis, such as if you are a personal brand, or it can be from your business to your audience.

Creating a group does require a fair amount of time and attention as you do need to be able to invest some time in paying attention to the group, moderating it, and supporting others in being able to participate in a healthy and enjoyable way as well. Furthermore, you will need to share the group frequently with incentives to get people to join it. However, once people have joined, your Facebook group can be as lucrative as your e-mail list. It is a great way to directly interact with your audience and provide value.

To create a group for your business, all you need to do is go to your Facebook page for your business and tap "*create group.*" Then, consider what you want the group to be used for and how that particular topic would be supportive of your audience and your brand. Once you have put the two together, you can go ahead and follow the steps to complete your group. You will have the opportunity to pick a name, write a description, create some group rules, and set the limitations on who can join, how, and who is allowed to approve new members. You can also add a cover photo for your group, and an announcement inviting and welcoming new members to the group. To adjust any further customizations, such as who may add to the group story or who can post and when, you can easily go into "Group Settings" and adjust them to accommodate for anything you feel will suit your group the best.

Early on, your group may feel slow and ineffective. However, as you continue to add to it and develop it, you will find that it becomes much more engaged and active. Typically speaking, individuals are more likely to interact and engage within a group than they are on your business page. Furthermore, the algorithm actually supports greater organic visibility with your group for group members than it does for your page with followers.

Chapter 6:
Paid Facebook Marketing

Creating paid advertisements for your Facebook page can be a powerful way to build your audience, reach more people, and have a greater impact with your campaigns. With Facebook, a greater amount of your audience will be reached through paid marketing because the algorithm is optimized to support your audience in seeing paid advertisements. This does not mean that you cannot build a strong engagement with an organic following, just that adding a paid element to your page can support you in having a greater reach and greater success.

That being said, you should refrain from using paid Facebook marketing until you have a strong idea of what your page's demographics and analytics look like. Every Facebook page comes with analytics that will automatically begin to provide you with detailed information about the demographics that are engaging most with your page. This is a great way to ensure that you are marketing to exactly the right people and that you are not wasting your budget. This information is detailed enough to begin using within 2-4 weeks following the creation of your Facebook page. You can access it on desktop browsers by going to your page and tapping "Insights." Along the sidebar of that page, you will see multiple options that you can look into, including "People." This one will tell you specifically who is following you and who engages with your content the most.

Once you have a strong idea of who your demographic is, Facebook offers many ways for you to begin interacting and engaging with your audience. You can choose many parameters for your advertisement, an objective, a budget, and the way it will look. It is important to understand that Facebook is better used for story marketing, sharing, and networking. Trying to facilitate hard sales on Facebook (i.e. "Toothbrushes - $2 each! Buy now!) will not work. People want to read, feel inspired, and take action.

Accessing Ad Manager

This is accessed by going to your Ads Manager, which can be located in the "Ad Center" section of your Facebook page, scrolling to the bottom and tapping "Create Ad" at the bottom of your screen.

Choosing Your Objective

Upon accessing your Ad Manager and selecting "Create Ad" you will be asked to choose your objective. Your objective section features 11 different objectives that you can choose, ranging from increasing brand awareness to encouraging people to download your application. You will want to choose the objective that best fits with the goal you have in mind for your advertisement.

After you have chosen your objective you will be asked to name the campaign. This name will only be visible by you or anyone else with access to your Ads Manager (so, anyone else that you have given advertising permissions to on your page.) You can also choose to create a "split test" which essentially means that you will create two completely different campaigns and promote them to see which campaign gets the best response. This can be a great way to determine what your audience responds to best so that you can refine your budget and marketing in the future to get the best responses. You can also choose to optimize your budget to ensure that your advertisement is delivered in the most optimal method possible.

Creating Your Ad – "Behind the Scenes"

With the objective and name in place, it is time to start building your advertisement.

This section allows you to outline your objective, offer, audience, placement, budget, and schedule. First, you will want to choose what your offer is and what you want most from the advertisement. The offer itself will be optional but does create a save feature on the ad so that viewers can save your advertisement and view it at a later date. You will be able to pick who your audience is (which should be the exact information you see in your page analytics,) choose where the ad will be placed on Facebook (choose "Automatic" if you do not know,) and then determine how much you want to spend and how long you want the advertisement to run for. Make sure that when you are choosing your budget you select the proper choice from the drop down menu.

Creating Your Ad – "The Visual"

The last thing that you will need to do before confirming your advertisement is to create the visual aspect of it. Here, you can choose what page you are advertising for, choose how you would like the ad to look, include any pictures and links or wording, and otherwise design the decorative visual aspects of your advertisement. Facebook now offers carousel, single image, single video, slideshow, and collection style formats. Each of these formats provides you with a different way to share images or videos with your audience. Make sure to pick the one that looks best based on what you are sharing. For example, if you have only one single image, do not pick the "carousel" look, as you will not have enough unique and high-quality images to fill each slot on the carousel!

Confirm Your Ad

Following the completion of all of the aforementioned aspects of your paid advertisement, you can tap "Confirm." You will then be asked to confirm the ad one more time, letting you confirm that all of the details in the advertisement are correct and that you are happy with the final outcome. Facebook will then review your ad and, as long as it meets their standards, approve it within 24 hours of you creating it. It will then begin circulating and reaching your audience to maximize your outreach and help you earn greater sales, exposure, or whichever other goal you aimed for!

Boosted Posts

Another form of advertisement that you can create with Facebook is known as a "boosted post." This promotion is created by simply tapping the "boost post" button at the bottom of any post on your page. Then, rather than having you create a paid advertisement with specific objectives and parameters, you can simply input your desired audience and boost the post to be seen by more people. This can be a great way to increase exposure and use your already-well-received posts as a way to create even more momentum in your business. Facebook will often recommend which ones to boost based on how other similar pages' boosted posts have performed and the amount of organic reach the post has already received.

Chapter 7:
Why Use Instagram in 2019

Instagram is a picture sharing social media platform that was purchased by Facebook in 2012. This purchase meant that the social media site began receiving many valuable updates that made it, even more, user-friendly for brands looking to maximize their earnings through the site. It also means that you can easily link your Facebook business and Instagram business accounts together so that you can easily share content between the two and manage them with ease.

In 2019, Instagram will continue growing as one of the best places for social media influencers to maximize their outreach and build their brands. While platforms like Facebook, Twitter, and YouTube are typically incorporated into influencer brands, Instagram is generally considered to be the most popular page of choice for influencers. As a business, this means that having an Instagram presence can support you in getting in front of influencers and having them promote your brand. Then, through their promotions, they can land viewers back to your page. Without a page, these viewers would have nowhere to refer back to when they see your product or service being enjoyed by their favorite influencers.

Aside from actually working together with influencers themselves, Instagram is actually a great way for brands to be discovered and become influencers themselves. The way Instagram is set up it is extremely easy for otherwise unassuming viewers to locate your brand and begin following you. Unlike Facebook which is typically through direct sharing or searching, Instagram can help you get discovered in a much larger way. All you need to do is use the right hashtags and as your ideal clients browse these hashtags they find you and thus, you are discovered by your ideal audience with minimal expenditure and effort.

That being said, there are key points to using Instagram effectively. In 2019, Instagram users will expect that any brand worth paying attention to will have extremely polished and professional looking feeds. Their images should be top quality, clean, and professional looking. They should also fit together creating a newsfeed that works as an overall advertisement itself. Colors that clash too much or an image that is hard to identify will muddy the feed and prevent users from wanting to follow you. Thus, if you are going to be on Instagram in 2019, you need to be ready to bring your A-game to the photo-sharing app. Fortunately, this is not nearly as hard as it sounds.

Business who will benefit the most from Instagram in 2019 are those that are catering specifically to individuals in the 18-35-year-old age range. These are the users who are on Instagram the most. It is also highly admired by those who are creative, artistic, or otherwise passionate about exquisite work. Whether you are sharing your own beautiful creations or taking exceptional images of otherwise "mundane" stuff (like a dentist chair,) having the right images and content will make a world of difference with your Instagram marketing.

Problems to Avoid

If you are marketing on Instagram, there are some problems you are going to need to avoid. These basic problems may seem like nothing much to you, but they can have a seriously dampening effect on your ability to effectively market and share your business with your audience.

One of the biggest problems that people face when marketing on Instagram is using hashtags that have been blacklisted. These are typically hashtags that have somehow been associated with something deemed inappropriate by Instagram. For example, they may be associated with an excessive number of pornographic posts, inappropriate language, bullying, or otherwise. You can avoid using these hashtags by following the steps in Chapter 8 to find proper hashtags that you *should* use when tagging your posts.

Another problem that many business users face includes wanting to purchase followers as a way to quickly build your platform. It is not uncommon to read about lengthy guides that advocate for this and direct you to platforms like Fiverr to pay someone a fee to receive "organic followers." What ends up happening when you do this is that Instagram quickly recognizes the irregular behavior and marks your account as spammy. It also results in your profile looking fake as it has many followers yet very little engagement. To both Instagram algorithms and your audience, this reflects poorly and prevents you from getting boosted up in the newsfeed. This means that you will be less likely to get seen in front of your desired audience.

Chapter 8:
Organic Instagram Marketing

Organic marketing on Instagram requires you to have a polished, well-created profile, and a great hashtag strategy. One of the greatest benefits of Instagram is how easy it is to use and how effortlessly you can get in front of your desired audience. In this chapter, we are going to look at how you can create an optimized Instagram profile if you do not already have one, or optimize your existing profile for marketing in 2019. We are also going to explore organic marketing strategies that you can begin taking advantage of right away to grow your following and engagement and begin receiving greater exposure to your target audience.

Creating and Optimizing Your Instagram Profile

The first part of being able to effectively build your brand on Instagram comes from having an optimized profile. If you already have a profile, the strategies in this section will support you in optimizing it so that your profile supports you in stronger marketing and outreach. If you do not, this section will support you in creating your profile.

Creating Your Account

If you are not yet on Instagram, you will need to create an account. The easiest way to do this is by creating your account from the mobile app, as Instagram is optimized for mobile usage and is not incredibly user-friendly on desktop. From the mobile application, which can be downloaded for free in the App Store or Play Store, you can see the option to "Sign In" or "Sign Up" from the main screen. If you tap "Sign Up" you will then be prompted to walk through the process of making a username, including your email, creating a password, then confirming your account.

For your username, make sure that you choose something as simple as possible. Ideally, your username and business name should be one in the same. However, it is important that you check for this username's availability across all platforms that you are desiring to use as you will want it to remain the same on all platforms. This will make it easier for you to be found. If you cannot find your exact username preference on all platforms be sure to choose an alternative that makes sense and is easy for your audience to identify. For example, instead of using "PieBakery1234567" which looks extremely unprofessional, you could switch it to "VancouverPieBakery" or "ThePieBakery" or something similar. Making sure that your username is easy to identify and remember will be important, so do not discredit this. On Instagram, your username *can* be changed, but you do not want to have to change it as this can be confusing to your followers.

Choosing Your Profile Picture

On Instagram, your profile picture cannot be blown up or seen close-up by your audience. This means that having a complex, blurry, overwhelming or confusing image here will actually take away from it and even drive your audience away to a more thought out profile. The best thing to put in your profile picture is your logo, as this makes it clear, easy, and identifiable. If you do not have a logo, consider doing a clean headshot, or an image of a very basic product with a clean white background.

Writing Your Bio

Your bio allows you to use 150 characters to tell people about who you are, what you do, and why they should be interested in following you. In this space, you can also include hashtags and tag other accounts. This gives you even more versatility when it comes to building out larger brand images, creating a hashtag that is specific to your brand, or otherwise identifying what is important and identifiable about your brand. In addition to being direct and clear, your bio should also include personality. This is the only piece of written content that your users will see from your profile unless they click directly on your images, so you want to make sure that you get across who you *really* are with this piece. You can also include emojis, which are extremely popular on Instagram. Including a few relevant emoji's that share your personality and amplify your profile is a great way to diversify your image to your audience and blend in with the Instagram scene.

In your bio, you can also include a link to your website or sales page, or any other accounts you may have on social media. Alternatively, you might consider using a linking service that allows you to store multiple links under one URL. Services such as LinkTree allow you to have one vanity URL that you can include on Instagram. Then, interested parties can tap that link and are taken to a list that will show them the many other links they can go to in order to see more about your business. This is a great way to link to other social media accounts as well as your website, link to your website as well as specific products or services that are currently being advertised, or otherwise.

Converting to A Business Account

Once you have your account created, you will want to convert it into a business account. Business accounts allow you to share more information, including your business e-mail address, your business location, business hours and information, and other business information. It also gives you access to analytics, promotions, and other features that will support you in sharing your business online.

To convert your account to a business account, simply go to "Settings" and tap "Switch to Business Account." Then, you will be able to switch your account over. In this process, you will see the opportunity to link your business Instagram account to your business Facebook page. If you have one, it is highly recommended that you do so. Connecting the two will allow you to easily cross-promote. Any promotions you make on Instagram or Facebook can effortlessly be displayed on the other platform as well, making the process of creating and managing paid promotions significantly easier. You can also increase your organic reach this way by creating a post on Instagram then "sharing" it to Facebook. This can also work with sharing posts to your Twitter account, meaning each post gets you a lot further.

Designing Your News Feed

Having an attractive news feed is essential for anyone who is seeking to have a strong business strategy in 2019. Your audience wants to see high quality, attractive, and well-organized images in your profile. You can do this on your own by imagining what each image looks like side-by-side, or you can use applications like PLANN, The Preview App, or others. These applications let you upload pictures into the application first to see what they look like side-by-side. You can also drag and drop the images around to make sure that your feed looks optimal. Then, you can include the caption and hashtags directly from the app. Once that is done, you can schedule the posts and have your feed fully automated as well as completely designed. These applications are not required, but they can be extremely helpful for businesses looking to have a strong profile and who do not want to have to hover over social media all hours of the day.

Choosing images for your news feed and arranging them is a three-step process: you need to choose and edit the image, write the caption, and hashtag the image. The best way to do this is to choose a high-quality image and, if you filter it, use a common set of filters that all of your images will use. That way, all of your filters, colors, and tones remain consistent on your page. Then, your caption should be either short and concise, or informative and engaging. Instagram users are not a big fan of reading large captions, so if you choose to do longer informative posts they do need to be highly engaging and interesting, and they should not be used too frequently. That way, you do not bore your audience or miss out on engagement opportunities. You should also use a lot of emojis, as these provide a "treat" for your reader's eyes, making it easier for them to read and more enjoyable as well. Lastly, you need to choose popular hashtags that are going to get your image seen. Each hashtag has the opportunity to get your photo in front of tens of thousands if not hundreds of thousands of new people. It is extremely important that you take great advantage of hashtags. Because of their importance, we have created their own section on tips and tricks below to make sure that you hack the hashtag game and really get the hang of it in a way that helps your page grow organically, and fast.

Hashtag Tips and Tricks

Hashtags on Instagram are how you get found. Naturally, you want to make sure that you are hashtagging effectively to make sure that you are getting found by all of the right people. This can take some time, practice, patience, and research, but once you discover the right techniques to get it down, hashtagging becomes effortless and Instagram becomes one of your best marketing tools on the net.

The first step in hashtagging properly is having a list or note on your phone where you store popular hashtags. Some people and apps might suggest that you pre-create hashtag "groups" that you can easily copy and paste into your photos, but as of 2018 this technique will actually result in Instagram pushing your image further down the feed as it is considered spammy and inauthentic by their algorithm. Instead, keeping a running list of the most popular hashtags and paying attention to the ones that get you the most views (and the ones that don't) is going to be your best bet. Any hashtags that are underperforming you can delete from your list. Any that are performing incredibly well should be kept. Most post planner apps and third-party Instagram analytic apps will teach you about how well each hashtag is working to help you find your best ones.

To choose how to compile your list, you can do two things: first, pick a popular hashtag and search it on Instagram. At the top of the search page, you will find "suggested hashtags" which will show you other popular and trending hashtags being used by the same community. Picking these and findings ones that are used more than 75,000 but less than 999,999 times will ensure that you get ones that are popular but not *too* popular. Any that are less than 75,000 are unlikely to be seen by a big enough audience. Any with more than 999,999 are being used so frequently that you can pretty much guarantee that your post will be rapidly drowned out by others using the same tag. Ones that are somewhere in between are a great area to fall into because they offer you a big audience, but not too big of a competition.

Another thing to consider is that Instagram will allow you to use up to 30 hashtags per comment. You do not want to put multiple comments with hashtags to increase this number as this will make your post look spammy and overwhelming. Instead, you want to keep it to 10-30 hashtags per post, ideally going into the 30 count. In these 30, use hashtags that are relevant to your picture and what you are sharing and that market to the right audience. You should also focus on being quite specific, as this helps people find you specifically. For example, "#fashion" would be far too broad, but "#customfashion," "#handmadefashion," "#highstreetfashion," "#everydayfashion," and other similar and specific hashtags are perfect. This means that people are looking for specifically what you have to offer, thus increasing your chances of being discovered by them. If you go too broad, not only will you be rapidly drowned out by the competition, but you will also have a large number of uninterested people viewing your pictures while looking for something else. Getting more specific maximizes your reach.

When you are hashtagging, rather than tagging the post itself within the caption, post and then tag in the comments. You want to tag your hashtag comment no more than 30-60 seconds within having your post up as this will ensure that your post gets engagement and gets seen. Waiting too long will actually result in your post being seen as "uninteresting," thus minimizing the number of people who see it. A good way to make this happen quickly is to go to your list of popular hashtags, create a custom group for that specific image beforehand, then copy and paste it. Then, you can delete this group and recreate a new one every time you go to post. This may seem like it takes a bit of work, but it will prevent Instagram from hiding your posts.

Lastly, make sure that if you are choosing hashtags from any method other than what Instagram recommends directly through their discover page and through the method listed above that you check it on Google. This will ensure that you are not accidentally using blacklisted hashtags which will actually result in your image being completely hidden from all newsfeeds as a way to prevent spam or inappropriate images being spread across the platform.

Engaging With Your Followers

Your followers are the ones boosting your profile, liking your pictures, and giving your profile credibility. The more followers you get, the more you need to engage with them. Doing this is an extremely simple way of organically building relationships with your audience and supporting them in remembering who you are. It also shows potential followers that you care and that if they support you that you will be genuinely interested in developing a relationship back with them.

One obvious way to engage with followers is to comment back whenever they comment on your content. You should also search your brand's specific hashtag if you have one and like and comment on anyone who posts specifically about your brand. These particular people are going out of their way to share your brand, so rewarding them with attention and interaction is a great way to show your gratitude and thank them for their support.

You should also spend some time each day scrolling popular hashtags that are relevant to your business. Liking and, more importantly, commenting on other peoples' posts is a great way to get seen and increase the number of people paying attention to your page. It is important that you use genuine comments in this situation. Many businesses have come under fire recently for using pre-canned, generic "We love your page! Check ours out, too!" type comments that are seen as inauthentic and ingenuine by their audience. This gives your brand a spammy feel and can actually take away from the relationships you are building with your audience.

Instagram stories, Instagram live, and IGTV are three other features that give you a great opportunity to interact with your audience in a more live-in-the-flesh manner. Stories are always a great way to offer interesting, behind-the-scenes snippets of your day to your audience so that they can feel as though they are seeing into your life and genuinely building a relationship with you. If you run a brand that is identified on its own, you can focus the story on your employees and the goings on at your store or company. Instagram stories also offer a unique feature to those with 10,000+ followers that allow you to attach links directly to your story. This means that you can advertise for a new product, service, blog post, or otherwise directly in your story and then inform watchers to "swipe up" to access the link and visit your link to purchase or further engage with your brand. This can be accessed by tapping the chain link icon in the top right corner of the screen when making stories and putting the link into the space provided. Again, this feature is only available to those with more than ten thousand followers.

Instagram live is a great way to offer live Q&A sessions, introductions, information, and other valuable, interesting, or entertaining tidbits to your audience in a way that allows you to directly communicate back and forth. Because it features your face and voice live on a video, it creates a more personalized and intimate connection between you and your audience.

IGTV is another great feature that was recently included. This particular feature works much like live but stays in the IGTV feed for 24 hours following your upload. It allows you to stay live for much longer, do more, and have a more professional look to your page. This is great for sharing tutorials, updating people on important happenings in your business, educating them, and otherwise sharing video-based marketing information in a more professional and new age manner.

Building A Strong Instagram Audience

Building your following on Instagram is generally the objective, but you want to make sure that you are building a strong, engaged, and large following as you go. The best way to do this is to take all of the tips provided in this chapter and practice them alongside *consistency*.

With Instagram, consistency is key. If you are not consistent in volume or quality, you will rapidly lose followers. You need to remain consistent in posting, engaging, and professional high-quality imagery if you are going to continue building your audience. You should also keep your hashtag list relevant and up-to-date and regularly check for trending hashtags in your community that you can jump on board with to benefit off of.

As long as you remain consistent, your audience will continue to grow and before you know it your page will be massive. Then, your Instagram sales channel will begin to grow and before you know it you will be earning a killing through your Instagram feed.

Chapter 9:
Paid Instagram Marketing

Paid marketing on Instagram works similarly to paid marketing on Facebook. One great aspect is that when you pay to market something on Facebook, you can actually push that same advertisement over to Instagram. This form of cross-promotion creates the opportunity to have the same budget and ad back-end settings monitoring a single advertisement across two platforms. Overall, this decreases the amount of work required on your end and maximizes your exposure.

Other than having the great ability to cross-promote between Instagram and Facebook, there are many other aspects of paid Instagram marketing that make it a great tool for reaching more followers, increasing your exposure and sales, and growing your business. Paid Instagram advertisements support your page in getting seen by many more individuals than it would if it were merely shared organically. That is not to say that organic marketing is not effective or widespread, because it certainly is. However, when done right, paid advertisements on Instagram can get you a larger guaranteed reach, thus making them highly effective and useful for you.

Types of Instagram Advertisements

Instagram features four types of advertisements: photo ads, video ads, carousel ads, and story ads. Each of these promotions are displayed on Instagram in a different way. Photographs will be static photographs with a call to action button that is displayed only once the interest party taps "like" on your picture. Video ads are the same. Carousel ads provide viewers with the opportunity to scroll to see all of your offers or photos of interest. Lastly, story ads are displayed between stories that are being viewed by your target audience.

The best way to get the most out of Instagram marketing is to use each of these different ad types on a regular basis. In particular, you need to make sure that you are using at least one form of news feed based advertisement (photo ad, video ad, or carousel ad) and the story advertisement. These different methods will ensure that you are being seen by your audience no matter where they are spending most of their time on this particular application.

Creating Your Instagram Advertisement

A fascinating aspect of building ads on Instagram is that it actually works exactly like creating an ad on Facebook, right down to using the built-in Ads Manager on Facebook. This means that everything you learned about in chapter 6 for creating Facebook ads will also walk you through the step-by-step process for creating an ad on Instagram.

The primary thing to pay attention to here is that when you are selecting which identity you want to advertise for (found in the Ad Settings page) you choose the identity of your chosen Instagram profile. Then, you go about designing the ad exactly as you would one for Facebook. At this rate, you can also choose to advertise on both Instagram *and* Facebook, or strictly Instagram. This is entirely up to you.

If you want to promote a post without going through the Ads Manager, you can also find your desired post to promote on Instagram (or create one) and then tap the "Promote" button beneath the image. There, you will be walked through the process of promoting the image directly through the Instagram application without ever having to access the Facebook Ads Manager.

Chapter 10:
Why Use YouTube in 2019

Video marketing is rapidly increasing in popularity, providing marketers with a unique opportunity to give personalized introductions to their brand, products, services, and other aspects of their business. Research has shown that video marketing is more effective than photographs and words because it gives viewers the unique opportunity to hear the voice, see the personality, and experience the brand in a way that photographs do not allow for. If you want to make the most out of video marketing, getting onto YouTube is essential.

YouTube is great because it caters to 59% of the popular who prefers watching video versus reading, and more than 3.25 billion hours of video are watched through YouTube on a monthly basis. The average viewer is between 18-49 years old, making this the perfect platform for marketers catering to a variety of different demographics.

The key with YouTube is understanding that just because you are on YouTube does not necessarily mean that you need to focus on expanding your YouTube following and subscribers. YouTube is a unique platform where you can focus specifically on developing your fanbase on YouTube itself, or you can use it as a unique tool in creating video marketing content for other platforms, such as Facebook and Twitter.

YouTube offers many unique assets to brands in a way that can seriously enhance credibility, interest, and authority. For example, having someone send you a video testimonial of your brand and uploading it to your YouTube account and then sharing it with your fans is a great way to share a more heartfelt explanation as to why your existing customers love your business so much. Alternatively, you can use YouTube as a way to share introductions to your business, products, and services and show your audience why *you* love your company so much, thus giving them a greater reason to love it more as well.

Establishing authority through YouTube can be done by creating powerful clips of you sharing valuable information about your industry. For example, say you run a photography company. You could use YouTube as a way to provide tips on how professional photographers can take better images, how they can edit better, and which software and programs are the best to use when it comes to editing their images. You can also provide the everyday person information and tips on how to take better images with their cell phones, better selfies, and other handy layman tips. Creating a page filled with advice, information, tips, and support is a great way to show that you know what you are doing and that you are happy to help others do just as well.

When it comes to YouTube, you can have your audience engage with you and stay connected with you directly through YouTube by having them subscribe and follow your content directly on YouTube, or you can have them find you elsewhere online. This means that YouTube is extremely supportive in building a native audience as well as building your audience elsewhere.

In essence, virtually everyone should be using video marketing as a strategy in 2019. That being said, incorporating YouTube is a great way to make sure that you are getting the most out of video marketing opportunities since the entire platform is dedicated to video itself. This means that you get the best support, opportunities, features, and algorithms to support you in being found. Furthermore, YouTube offers opportunities for you to make money through advertisements, thus increasing your exposure *and* earning you a small income through the app itself. With that being said, it is a great social media platform for virtually every business to get on. With the right creativity and focus, YouTube could be one of your best marketing tools to date.

Problems to Avoid

YouTube has a few problems that you could run into if you are not focused on avoiding them effectively. Namely, not focusing on developing your YouTube channel properly can seriously hold you back. Building space for your brand on YouTube allows you to customize your page, organize it, and optimize your viewer's experience. Or, you can simply throw everything on there and hope it sticks. Obviously, you want to use the available settings to create a fun and enjoyable experience. Taking advantage of the settings and features available to you will ensure that you have a great page that people are eager to browse and watch on.

You also need to avoid relying on viral videos. The truth is, nothing can guarantee that a video will go viral. The trick is that rather than waiting for this to happen, you aim to make every video viral *worthy*. That way, the video is extremely high quality and ready for all viewers, and it has the potential to go viral. This does not guarantee that it will, but it will certainly support you in getting great viewership nonetheless.

Another problem to avoid is not paying attention to your analytics. YouTube will tell you exactly what your viewers like, what they are responding best to, and who it is exactly that is responding. Paying attention to these analytics can support you in creating videos that cater specifically to your audience. Then, they are more likely to enjoy more of what you post and remain followers. Just putting up content because you want to create it and not necessarily because your audience wants to see it can seriously inhibit your viewership and stunt your page growth.

Chapter 11: Organic YouTube Marketing

YouTube is actually one of the easiest social media platforms for organic marketing. Unlike others which place fairly equal emphasis on both organic and paid marketing strategies, YouTube was originally based around organic marketing for quite a long time. In fact, many of the organic marketing strategies that made YouTube so great in the beginning are still vital staples in YouTube marketing right now and are expected to remain so through all of 2019.

Organic YouTube marketing goes through a four-step process. This process includes having an optimized YouTube channel that remains up to date, filming high-quality videos, optimizing your videos with proper SEO, and marketing your videos. Unlike other social media platforms where you simply hit "post" and you are done, YouTube does require a few additional shares in order to get your videos in front of the eyes of as many as possible. That being said, when done properly the amount of exposure that you stand to gain from a single video, never mind a well-put-together channel in its entirety, is massive. So, let's get started on discovering how you can optimize your organic YouTube marketing strategies to stay up to date and relevant with your business in 2019.

Creating and Optimizing Your YouTube Channel

If you do not yet have a YouTube channel, this guide will walk you through starting one from scratch and optimizing it for 2019 standards. If you do already have a channel, you can still use this guide and measure your present channel against its standards to ensure that you are optimized for maximum viewer reach and subscribers.

Create Your Account

The first step is for you to create your YouTube channel. This is fairly simple. Just go to YouTube.com and choose the "Sign Up" button in the top right corner of the screen. There, you will be walked through the process of signing up for a YouTube account with your Google e-mail. If you do not yet have a Google e-mail delegated for your business, it would be a good idea to create one to use for this process. This will ensure that all aspects of your account remain business-oriented. Creating your account is easy: simply follow the steps, go to your e-mail inbox and "confirm" your account. Then, you have a YouTube account!

Branding Your Account

With your account successfully created, it is time to brand it to your business. To do this, log in to your YouTube account, and go to "My Channel" from the left sidebar menu.

Immediately, a pop up will arise asking you to input some information to create your channel. Before inputting any information to create the channel, look to the bottom of the pop-up box. There, you will see an option that says "Use a business or other name." Select that option and then you will be taken to another screen where you can input the branded account's name. Now, your account will be optimized for your company.

Branding Your Profile

Your channel is now successfully named after your business, but that is not enough. For a channel to really be considered legitimate and worthy in 2019, you need channel art. This includes having a professional, high-quality profile image and a cover for your profile that is also high quality and professional. For your profile photo, you can use a clear headshot of yourself or, preferably, a high-resolution image of your logo. Channel art can easily be made and branded on any standard image editing application, such as Canva. There, you can input your 2560 x 1440 px image. Make sure that you choose an image that will have a high quality, identifiable center as this is the only portion that will be viewed on mobile. You can see which part of the image will be seen on mobile when you upload the channel art. It is essential that you optimize this art for mobile as most of your viewers will be watching from their handheld devices, so you want your page to look professional and clean-cut.

Once your branded images are in place, you can customize your "About" page. Simply tap the "About" page from your channel and select the "Edit" option. Then, you can input information about what your business is, who it serves, and what your story is. You can also give potential viewers an idea of what to expect from your page and where else they can find you online.

Filming an Introduction Video

The primary page for your profile offers the opportunity for you to create an introduction video for anyone who lands on your page. This video will play automatically upon them landing on your profile, meaning that they can listen to your introduction while browsing, or opt to watch it as they learn more about who you are. Ideally, this video should be 60 seconds or less. It needs to be direct, to-the-point, and concise while also being an accurate representation of what your brand is all about.

Initially, this 60-second clip should be a professional, high-quality video of you introducing yourself and your brand to your new audience member. The minimum shooting quality for a YouTube video should be 1080p, but 4k films are preferred going into 2019. 4k films offer an exceptionally high-resolution film and the majority of handheld devices are now viewing and filming in 4k, meaning that you need to keep up with the technology to stay relevant and on top.

As you grow, many brands will go ahead and use this introduction as a way to quickly introduce new or popular products or services to their audience. So, rather than introducing your company name and mission statement, you could easily make a catchy and attractive short 30-45 second clip of your best-seller and place it here. This will give your audience something to quickly become attracted to and thus become interested in learning more about who you are and what you have to offer. Then, you can have a playlist dedicated to introducing your company and your mission so they know who you are. Or, they can simply pop over to your "About" page to get a better idea and then scroll your playlists to find other interesting and attractive video content. This is not necessary early on, but you may wish to use this strategy to keep your page fresh and your audience engaged as you grow.

Filming Videos for Your Channel

Filming for your YouTube channel is not nearly as intimidating as it may sound. In fact, it can be extremely fun to do, especially when you know your content well enough and you are passionate about sharing it with others. That being said, there are many standards that need to be met going into 2019 to keep your film competitive against others that will certainly be uploaded. If you want to be amongst those actually ranking well and begin watched, you need to have strong YouTube standards for your own film and an understanding of how to be competitive in the first place. Let's explore what you need to have a great film for your channel.

Film Quality

Filming standards for YouTube have changed drastically in the past few years. Not too long ago, point-and-shoot digital cameras that filmed in 360p or, at best, 720p. In fact, many original YouTubers became famous using their webcams which lagged, glitched, and had extremely pixelated and poor quality filming all around.

Nowadays, with video marketing taking off more than ever before and so many people wanting to take advantage of the video marketing trends for their growing businesses, standards have raised significantly. Ideally, every film should be shot in 4k. At a very minimum, 1080p. These films need to be taken in the most professional settings possible. This can seem intimidating at first, but once you grow used to filming this way you will find it to be much easier to do and it becomes second nature.

What Your Viewers Are Looking For

What you need to aim for when creating videos is great film quality, attractive imagery, and interesting information. The videos that end up trending or going viral are almost always ones that are short, informative, inclusive of subtitles, and entertaining. Some longer videos do go viral, though these are generally less common to do so. Ideally, you want to aim for every single video to go viral as this is how you can ensure that you are filming with the highest quality of standards there is.

There are eight primary video types that are popular on YouTube. They include customer testimonials, on-demand product demonstrations, tutorials, thought leader interviews, reviews and case studies, live videos, vlogs, and event videos. While you can certainly incorporate all of these into creating a strong YouTube channel, the ones that are most likely to be shared amongst other social media platforms and go viral are typically tutorials and product demonstration videos.

Filming these videos requires some planning. Ideally, you want natural light, a 4k camera, a quiet environment, and a clean background. You should be well presented and ready to discuss anything that needs to be said or shared, should speaking be involved in your video. This will ensure that your filming conditions are proper and that your video visually holds up to the standards required by the internet in 2019.

Making Your Videos More Attractive

For content, there are many ways that you can optimize the content in your video to be more viewer-friendly. Having the content broken up into small segments, such as breaking a video down into steps or using header slides to break up parts of your demonstration is a great way to cut up an otherwise longer video to make it more digestible for your viewer. You can also use various film and photograph effects to create an interesting image that is both informative and fun to watch. For example, many cooking videos will have fun effects where the chef snaps their fingers and suddenly all of the potatoes are sliced or the hard-boiled eggs are peeled. Adding unique and entertaining effects such as this is not too hard (you can use

YouTube itself for tutorials!) and can make your video far more interactive and entertaining for your audience. Then, you are more likely to be watched and shared, thus maximizing your viewership and subscribers.

Optimizing Your Videos for SEO

The next thing that you need to do for your YouTube videos to rank well and be seen by others is to optimize them for SEO. SEO, or search engine optimization, is necessary because YouTube itself works like a search engine in providing videos to their viewers. This also makes your video more likely to pop up on other search engines, such as Google or Yahoo, when potential viewers search for content just like yours.

SEO is an extremely simple tool that you can incorporate into your videos through their title, description, tags, category, thumbnail, and subtitles. In the following steps, we will introduce how this works. Remember, it is essential that you take advantage of as many different ways of being recognized as you possibly can. Not doing so can result in you being missed, meaning many others who are paying attention will rise to the top. Incorporating as many strategies into being seen as possible will secure your position in the top ranking and help you get seen by as many people as possible.

Optimizing Your Title and Description

Your title and description feature many written words that are not included in other areas of your video. Since YouTube is video-based, many search engines cannot actually decipher what is *in* the video so they rely on the title and description to determine whether it fulfills the needs of their audience or not.

Optimizing your title and description requires you to use keywords that your audience is most likely to use. Your title will be the first thing that people read when seeing your video, so having it clear and optimized for SEO will also make it more clear and attractive to any potential viewer scrolling the list of available videos.

With your title, you want to keep it to 60 characters or less so it is not cut off on the browsing list. You also want it to be interesting and attractive, yet descriptive and clear. For example "Watch me unbox my Sephora brushes!" is more attractive than "Sephora brush unboxing." As you can see, the first one is clear but also interesting, whereas the second is clear but pretty boring. Keeping it fun and entertaining can encourage viewers to actually view the video.

With your description, being clear and incorporating as many keywords as possible while still keeping your description sounding professional and well put together is important. In other words, you do not want to use so many keywords that it sounds forced, but you do want to use enough that it can be discovered by search engines. Keep the popular keywords as "necessary" to add, and the others as "if possible" when adding. That way, your best keywords are included and, if you can, you add any additional ones for greater reach. You also want to make sure that you add a call to action in your description. For example "Subscribe to my channel!" "Check out more of our awesome products at www. example .com!" or otherwise. Giving your interested viewers somewhere to go so that they can learn more is a great way to market your business through YouTube!

Finding out which keywords you need to emphasize on is fairly simple. Using an application like Google Trends is a great way to discover what keywords are trending in your industry. Be sure to check in regularly as these keywords may change as trends change and you do not want to be left in the dust.

Optimizing Your Tags

Using your main keywords as tags in your video is helpful, also. This will ensure that when search engines are crawling for the video's tags they locate the keywords once again, thus maximizing your chances of being found. You should use a mixture of short and longer keywords here as this will be optimal in helping you get your page discovered!

Optimizing Your Category

Each video has the opportunity to be placed in a category on YouTube. You can access this option under "Advanced Settings" on your video. Placing your video in the appropriate category is great for SEO because it makes it even clearer to search engines that they are choosing the right video when they offer yours as the best option for their viewers. Make sure that you choose a category that fits your video the best so that you are not being misrepresented by the category and thus being skipped over.

Optimizing Your Thumbnail

Again, *everything* about film and photography is high quality in 2019. If your thumbnail is not high resolution, YouTube will likely skip over showing you to their audience because they know that their audience likely will not click to your video. The best way to optimize your thumbnail on your video is to custom create one specifically for your video. Applications like Canva offer YouTube video cover templates that you can use and customize to your branding so that your thumbnails remain high resolution and consistent. This is a great way to have your image both attractive to your ideal audience *and* to search engines, including the native YouTube search bar.

For your thumbnail, make sure that you save the image to your computer with a keyword in it. So, instead of saving it as "img234.jpeg" save it as "makeup.jpeg" as this will also be viewed by the search engine. Having the entirety of the image optimized will ensure that it is attractive, likely to be clicked, and easy for the search engine to display your video and channel altogether.

Optimizing Your Subtitles

Subtitles are great for two reasons. First and foremost, they make viewing your video easier. For those who are hard of hearing or those who are in a situation where they cannot actively watch with sound, having subtitles is a great way to ensure that they can still watch your video in that very moment without having to guess what you are saying or doing. This means that you are being considerate to your audience and that you are far more likely to get views.

Secondly, subtitles are written words. Search engines can crawl through the words written within the subtitles and quickly determine whether your video actually meets the search terms of their users or not. If they do, then you are more likely to get seen. In other words, this is a great way to up your keyword count, especially if you use a lot of keywords in the audio part of the film itself.

Marketing Your Videos and YouTube Channel

YouTube channels really flourish when you take the time to actually market your videos. Unlike Facebook which automatically shows it to your audience on the feed, they regularly scroll or Instagram shows it when one of the hashtags you used is searched, YouTube only gives a notification to your subscribers that your video was viewed. Simple notifications are the most likely to be ignored, making it unlikely that your video will reach a high organic viewership rating if you do not take the action to get it out there.

A great way to market your YouTube channel includes sharing your finished video to your other social media accounts and including it in your email marketing list. You can also encourage your followers to share the video, helping it get out there even more and reach an even larger number of people.

If you have a website or a blog, you can also include your latest videos there. Doing a quick blog update about your latest video or having the film embedded somewhere on your website is a great way to have it viewed by others, thus bringing them over to your channel. You can also include a little YouTube icon on your website itself, showing your website visitors that you are on YouTube and encouraging them to hop over to your YouTube page to begin checking out your video content.

You can also post your video on Q&A sites if you find anywhere your video would be relevant. For example, say you find a forum where people are talking about event planning. If someone has a question and you have a video that perfectly answers that question, you can include a short written answer with a link to your video that explains it better. This would then encourage the individual asking to go over to your YouTube, as well as anyone else who may have a similar question or curiosity. This is not only a great marketing technique, but it also drives up SEO as the more your video's link is shared, the more popular the video itself becomes and therefore the more search engines will bump it up the list so that it can be seen by others with similar searches.

Collaborating with other YouTubers is another great way to market your channel. This way, you can share each other's audiences by marketing the video to each of your audience's respectively. This means that they gain access to your audience and you gain access to theirs, thus supporting you in increasing your viewership and vice versa.

Lastly, it is always important to engage with viewers on *social* media. Just like you would on any other platform, make sure to comment back to those who take the time out to comment on your videos. This will ensure that they see that you care and that you are listening to what they have to say. It will also increase engagement rating on your video, thus driving it up the ranking list even more. Furthermore, engaging back with your audience gives you the opportunity to get to know them better and have a greater idea of what they are interested in and what videos they prefer. Then, you can easily begin creating more content that they are likely to enjoy, thus allowing you to optimize your entire YouTube strategy for your viewer specifically.

Chapter 12:
Paid YouTube Marketing

Like all other great social media platforms, YouTube offers a great paid marketing system for you to increase your viewership and market your channel and business directly on YouTube.

YouTube has a great built-in analytics system that allows you to understand your viewers better, thus helping you determine what your video should be about, who to market it to, and what results you can expect to gain from it. There are a few key differences when marketing on YouTube as compared to anywhere else because you will need to create a video specifically for your campaign. This has obvious differences from creating a post with an image and sharing it as it requires more planning and attention to visual detail to make sure that the video is actually likely to gain traction with your target audience. That being said, when done properly, paid YouTube marketing is an extremely powerful tool that can support you in maximizing viewership and getting a massive amount of exposure regarding your business, upcoming or ongoing sales, new products, or anything else that you may desire to advertise in this highly modern and 2019-optimized manner.

Measuring YouTube Analytics

YouTube will provide you with great analytics on all of your videos. These analytics tell you about important information such as audience retention, watch time, traffic sources, demographics, and engagement reports. These analytics will support you in understanding what type of content is the most popular for your particular audience, who is watching it, and for how long. With this information, you can create a video campaign aligned with your most popular content, targeted at your unique demographic, and customized to the perfect length to ensure that your viewers actually watch the video all the way through. As long as you pay attention and measure for these three particular analytics, you can ensure that you have all the information about your audience that you will need to plan the best campaign that will get you the best results.

Types of Advertisements

YouTube offers two different types of advertisements: video discovery ads and in-stream ads. Video discovery ads are shared at the top of the list when viewers browse for content like yours or match your targeted demographic. In-stream ads are displayed within other videos, shown as the ads that occur at the beginning of most YouTube videos or throughout the center of, particularly long ones. Both are powerful at engaging your audience, though in-stream ones are more likely to get viewed because they are pushed to your audience whereas video discovery ads remain at the top of the list and can easily be skipped over.

With video discovery ads, your key point of being able to attract your target demographic and get them to actually watch your film comes from having interesting content that does not feel like an infomercial, and an attractive title that makes them eager to click. For example, promoting a 3-5 minute tutorial video with a call to action during and at the end of the video is a great video to promote here. Paired with a great title, this video will likely gain views. Promoting a 3-5 minute sales pitch, however, will not warrant you any significant results no matter how interesting the title is because most viewers in 2019 are tired of hard sales pitches.

For in-stream ads, you have about 5 seconds to really capture the attention of your audience before they click "skip" or forget about your content altogether once the video they intended to watch starts. If you can catch their attention, however, through interesting commentary and imagery, then you can retain their view and they will likely choose to skip over to your page or complete your call-to-action when prompted.

Choosing Your Objective

Deciding how to plan your campaign requires you to determine what exactly you want to gain from your campaign. In other words, what is your objective? You can easily promote a well-created video that you have already done by simply editing in a few slides that include a call to action. Alternatively, you can create a video specifically for this campaign by choosing what your objective is and planning the entire content around that objective.

For example, say your idea is to promote your event planning business for the upcoming wedding season in the summer. You could easily create a fun video displaying a simple DIY wedding project tutorial, then cut to a scene where you say something like "Not interested in doing it yourself? Then leave it to us at Wedding Planners! We know exactly what to do for your special day, saving you the time and hassle. Save your DIY projects for Christmas, hire us instead!" This makes your video both informative and fun, inviting any DIY-interested wedding parties to hop over to your channel and see what other tutorials they can learn from for their own weddings. This means that you get viewed and shared. It also means that for those who are uninterested in doing it themselves but who are interested in hiring someone, they have found an interactive, informative, and supportive wedding planner for their upcoming wedding. This means that you can successfully attract and retain *both* potential audience members, maximizing your own viewership and supporting you in getting far better results from your ads.

Once you know what it is that you are aiming to do, whether it be to gain customers,

138

increase viewers, get people to download your app, or otherwise, you can easily create a fun, informative, and entertaining video that encourages your potential audience to take action. Thus, your marketing strategy is deemed effective and you can successfully convert ad viewers into customers.

Filming Your Advertisement

If you are going to film a fresh video for your advertisement, you need to make sure that it fills all of the same requirements as any other YouTube film would. The film should be in 4k high resolution filming quality with a great background, great lighting, and a clear and natural speaker sharing your company on the film.

You also need to make sure that the first five seconds of your video is extremely interesting, attractive, and catchy. This is how you can make sure that your audience enjoys what they see and remains interested enough to watch the rest of the ad without simply skipping it to see the video they desired to watch in the first place.

If you are unsure as to how you can film a great advertisement film, consider looking up some samples on YouTube. Watch several videos in your niche and take account of what advertisements come up as you watch. This way, you can see exactly which ones catch your attention and which ones you do not care for and are eager to skip. This will give you a good idea of what your audience is feeling when watching videos, also. The ones that draw you in and keep you wanting to watch more are great quality and are ones that you should consider and learn from when making your own. The ones that you want to skip quickly should also be analyzed to understand *why* you wanted to skip so quickly.

Remember that in 2019, everyone wants a personal connection. The standard infomercial style ads, ones that look like bland or over-used television ads, and otherwise impersonal ads are no longer having the same impact on viewers. Video marketing is taking off for two very specific reasons: *personality* and *intimacy*. With video marketing, your audience gets to see and interact with the personality of your brand and get a feel for who you really are. They also get an intimate view of what you do or what you are selling, thus showing them far more than a static picture that lacks any "life." If you can incorporate these into your video marketing strategy, you will be far more likely to retain viewers and receive a positive return on your investment.

Creating Your Campaign

The last step for YouTube marketing is actually creating your campaign! For this, you need to first upload the video to your YouTube channel. Then, you need to go to your Google AdWords account (or create one if you do not yet have one) and select the "Campaign" option. There, you can paste the URL to your campaign video.

Once you have done that, you can add a headline and description for your video. This is what is going to show up in search results, so make sure to include keywords and keep it clear and interesting.

Then, you want to choose the objective. This is where Google will send viewers if they choose to click on the ad to follow your call to action. Ideally, this link should coincide with your call to action. So, if you are talking about a specific product, make sure the link takes them to that specific product on your website and not just your website itself. You can also send people to your YouTube channel if you want to get more subscribers or have more views on your other videos.

Next, you need to set your daily budget. This is how much you want to spend each day on advertising your video. Google will give you a recommended daily budget, but you can set a custom one as well. You can also choose to set a maximum cost-per-view (CPV) if you desire. Note that in doing so, you may limit your viewership. The standard CPV is $0.06.

Lastly, you need to choose your target audience. This target should be customized based on the demographics of those who are showing the most engagement and viewership on your channel. This way, you are targeting those who are already proving to be interested in what you have to offer. The only thing left to do after this is to review your ad terms and approve the advertisement. Google will then check over it to make sure it is appropriate, then it will be shared out on YouTube as your paid ad campaign!

Chapter 13:
Why Use Twitter in 2019

Incorporating Twitter into your social media strategy is an important way to ensure that you gain maximum exposure for your business in 2019. Twitter offers many different benefits to users, particularly in increasing exposure and creating a channel for more of your potential audience to locate you and thus land on your website so that they can purchase from your company.

One way that Twitter marketing really has a powerful impact on businesses is in the fact that it is considered to be a social currency in the online social media world. This means that because people think the application is "cool" they use it, and anyone who is on it is considered cool as well. Anyone who is not on it is likely considered to be behind or obsolete.

Another great thing is that Twitter is an open form of social media, meaning that anyone can see and interact with your profile.

Unlike other social media platforms that create closed or private profiles for users, Twitter allows anyone to locate you and discover you and, thus, follow your link off to anywhere else you desire to take them. In fact, statistics show that 47% of the people who land on Twitter profiles with links will actually follow those links to see what that person is sharing. Twitter is loaded with potential customers who are looking for products or services just like the ones that you are offering, and who are actively willing to locate you elsewhere based on your links provided.

Twitter actually optimizes their platform for marketing through their extensive analytics and all of the data they share with businesses in regards to their target audiences. This means that as a marketer, you can gain a massive amount of insight on your audience through the Twitter platform. This information is obviously highly valuable for helping you target a greater audience on Twitter, but it can also support you in targeting your audience elsewhere. Mixing together the extensive analytics that you gain from Twitter and those that you gain from other platforms that you are active on can give you a massively accurate insight to your audience overall, thus helping you choose marketing strategies, identify and target your audience, and maximize your exposure in all areas of the social media world, including Twitter.

As of 2018, roughly 1.3 billion people are registered to use Twitter. Of all of the businesses in the United States of America, 65.8% of them are active on Twitter and are using it to market to their target audience which may just happen to be the same audience that you are targeting. If you want to have competitive potential and maximize your exposure while showing that you are better than your competitors, a presence on Twitter is a must.

Problems to Avoid

A lot of talk goes on about how Twitter is not necessarily the best platform for reaching your audience through. Many have made allegations that "Twitter is dying" or becoming obsolete. The reality is, Twitter is still a highly popular form of social media and people everywhere are maximizing exposure and profits from Twitter for their businesses. The majority of those who are claiming that Twitter is obsolete are failing to understand that Twitter does come with a learning curve since it's look and usage is quite different from other platforms. Avoiding this problem largely comes from taking the time to understand Twitter and use it effectively so that you can actually reach your marketing objectives with this platform.

Another thing that people regularly struggle with on Twitter is having their entire feed filled with self-promotional talk. The entire purpose of Twitter is to be a *collective* conversation shared by thousands of people. If you want to get in on the conversation, you need to converse about things that others are actually interested in. Sharing about your business and self-promoting is completely acceptable, as long as you are not overdoing it. Consider a real-life conversation, for example. If you were talking to a group of 10 people and 5 of those people were actively engaging in mutual conversation while the other 5 were simply saying "Look at my new product!" "I am the best!" "Check out my new service!" "Look at my new blog post!" can you guess who would be paid most attention to? The initial five would be sharing and conversing with *each other* while the other five would be having individual conversations with themselves as no one else listened. If you want to take advantage of Twitter, especially in 2019 where the *social* aspect of social media is growing, you have to learn to amplify your online social skills. You will learn more about that in the following two chapters.

Lastly, automated marketing is a powerful tool that should be used in many circumstances to support your outreach efforts. That being said, automated direct messages on Twitter that are used to thank people for following them are tacky and ineffective. In most cases, people will feel that the message is ingenuine and spammy, and it may even result in you getting unfollowed once again. If you want to take advantage of automated marketing for Twitter, look to automatic and scheduled posts, not automatic direct messages. If you ever do decide to message someone, keep it focused on being personalized and custom-written, not generic and robotic sounding.

Chapter 14:
Organic Twitter Marketing

Building your following on Twitter using organic marketing is a great way to take advantage of this free platform and the many free services it offers users to maximize your exposure and create stronger customer relationships. However, as you read about in chapter 13, Twitter does have a learning curve that needs to be endured before you can really get the hang of it. That being said, once you take the time to understand the purpose of Twitter, how people engage on it, and how it actually works, Twitter can be a great platform for virtually anyone to grow their business rapidly.

There are many ways that you can use Twitter to market your business. In this chapter, we are going to discuss seven unique ways that you can use organic marketing on Twitter. These ways will support you in understanding how to get involved in the platform, as well as how to optimize it for your business going into 2019.

Creating and Optimizing Your Twitter Profile

The first thing you need to do to get active on Twitter is to have a Twitter account. If you already have one, this section will help you optimize your profile for 2019. If you do not, this section will help you create a brand new optimized profile that will help you take advantage of Twitter for 2019.

Create Your Username

Once you go to the Twitter page and start the sign-up process by inputting your e-mail and password, you will need to choose your username. As with all of your other social media accounts, it is necessary for you to choose the same username that you are using elsewhere. Keeping your username uniform across all platforms will ensure that you are easy to find by your followers.

If you do not yet have any other accounts, make sure you use something easy to identify and recognizable. It should also be easy to spell. Twitter allows you to use only 15 characters for your username, making it one of the most restrictive usernames across all social media platforms. For that reason, you may want to make your Twitter username *first* and then secure it on other platforms that you plan to create a presence on. That way, you can ensure that you are using the same name everywhere.

Note that your username on Twitter is permanent, so you cannot change it once you have your account created. Make sure it is something that you are willing to commit to as there is no going back once it is created.

Choose A Profile Photo

The next part of your page that you need to create is your profile photo. Your profile photo will be seen next to every Tweet, Retweet, comment, and other interaction you make on Twitter. For this reason, choosing something that is easy to identify is important. Ideally, your logo would be a great choice as it will help your audience recognize your logo and thus it supports your brand in becoming more easily recognized. Alternatively, you can choose a clear and focused headshot, or any other clear and clean image that represents your company well.

Write Your Bio

The bio on your page supports a 160 character bio that will help you introduce who you are, what you are doing, and why people should check out your link or follow your page. It is important that you keep your bio both informative and personalized. You do not want to use something generic like "Cheese factory located in Idaho, USA." Instead, you would want to use something like "The cheesiest cheese factory in the eastern states, located in Idaho, USA!" Using something quirky and informative will ensure that your followers know exactly who you are and what they are looking at, but also that they are engaged, interested, and already beginning to understand your brand's personality.

Pick A Header Image

Twitter users are able to put a header image at the top of their profiles that personalizes the account even more. This is also a prime marketing space for giving a great image that markets your best products or services. Photographs of events you have hosted, products, or of your employees all standing together are great for this space. You can also use an application like Canva to create a professional and clean-looking graphic image with text that would allow you to share your motto or slogan, or otherwise, share an important piece of bite-sized information with your followers. Ideally, you should change this image from time to time to keep it fresh and new for your audience.

Pinning A Tweet

On Twitter, you can have one Tweet that is pinned at the top of your timeline. This is the first Tweet that your viewers will see upon landing on your page, so make sure that it is something important and useful to pay attention to. This could be anything from your latest offer to the most recent news you have available about your company. Once you have published a standard Tweet, simply tap "Pin to your profile page" on the Tweet itself from the "More" option and it will be pinned. You can change this pinned Tweet any time your latest offer or current events change so that your audience can easily see what the latest news is for your business. Once you have pinned your Tweet, you have successfully created an optimized profile for Twitter!

Getting Your Page Verified

In 2019, a lot of fake or non-serious businesses will arise to attempt to make a quick buck. This is a growing trend that has been happening for a couple of years now and it is expected to get even worse in 2019. What happens is companies come out of the woodwork, buy a large amount of cheap stock off of wholesale markets, and sell them for inexpensive online. These companies are generally selling poor quality products and rarely have a customer service team to resolve any complaints which are made by their audience. It does not take long for them to accrue a large amount of negative complaints and then essentially fall off the scene. For those who feel this is the way to go, all the power to them. However, if you want a sustainable long-term business, customer service and quality need to be at the top of your list of priorities.

To ensure that your audience recognizes that you are serious about the services and products you offer and that you are focused on quality and customer service, getting your page verified is important. This can set you aside from others by proving that you are serious about what you do and that you are willing to put in the extra work to prove it by having your account verified. To a potential customer, this can be the difference between going to your link to see what products or services you offer, or clicking away for fear of getting sucked into another pop-up business that will be gone in a few months.

To get a verification mark on your account, you need to fill out some forms for Twitter and submit them. These forms will allow Twitter to ensure that you are a real person who is really in business, or who is really who they say they are, and that you have the best interest of Twitter users in mind. You can find the forms by going to Twitter's website, heading into your account settings, and tapping "Request to verify an account." Here, you will need to let Twitter know why you want your account verified, who you are and what you represent, and what your mission is. They also want to know if you have any other websites or social media accounts as this gives Twitter a way to prove your claims against your existing online presence to make sure that you are who you say you are and that they are making a good judgment call in verifying your account.

Using Video Marketing on Twitter

Video marketing was once challenging to do on Twitter, but more recently they have begun optimizing the platform to be inclusive of video marketing strategies. On these videos, you can include anything that you would in any other form of video marketing films. You can share information, entertainment product demonstrations, educational content, or otherwise to engage your audience and interest them. You can also go live on Twitter, sharing real-time information or demonstrations, or even engaging in a live Q&A call with your audience so that you can answer any questions that they may have and speak with them directly. As with other social media platforms, this form of live interaction with your audience is a great way to show them that you care and to put a face directly on your company.

If you have a company that features many different employees, you might consider giving trusted employees access to the Twitter account using Twitter teams (explained later in this chapter,) so that they can also share live video footage of the goings on in your company. This can be a great way to introduce the many different faces of your team and support your audience in feeling a greater relationship with your brand. It provides a unique and personalized conversation that has been lost in the online space but is rapidly growing in popularity once again.

Having a Post Schedule

Posting regularly is important. For Twitter, you should likely have a post schedule that reminds you when you need to post and how often. Applications like Buffer and Hootsuite are a great way to create Tweets in advance and share them to your profile. That being said, you will also need to personally log on and engage with others through your account as well. Each day new trends and conversation topics are arising and you simply cannot predict all of them and account for them in advance through these post schedulers. Nothing will compare to actually actively joining in the live conversation on a daily basis so that you can create updated Tweets that match the daily trends.

So, if you want to have a post schedule the best way to do it would be to have about three schedule posts that go out each day that you can schedule in advance. These should be conversation-focused but not overly focused on trends as the trends you schedule to talk about may be outdated by the time your post comes out. These more general posts should still be informative and engaging, but should also be created in a way where they can add to the daily conversation in general.

Then, you should log in each day and personally engage in the daily trends, even if just for a few minutes. This will ensure that your account stays rich with activity that is both fulfilling and on-trend. That ensures that your account stays relevant, that your audience always has stuff to read about your business, and that you are not losing relevancy by talking about outdated trends or missing out on trends altogether.

Taking Advantage of Twitter Teams

If you run a business with employees, or even if you are a one-person company with a virtual assistant, creating Twitter teams can be a great way to ensure that you do not have to single-handedly manage your Twitter account for your business. In companies with a larger number of employees, having Twitter teams can be a great way to get everyone involved, to manage customer service inquiries that come in through Twitter, and to do "Twitter takeovers" where one employee hops on and Tweets for a while before another team member takes over, later on, to begin sharing. This creates a powerful dynamic for your account, giving viewers more to look forward to and helping them create rich relationships with the various members of your team.

Twitter teams can be created by using TweetDeck. Up to 200 team members can Tweet to your business account with

TweetDeck, making it a great application to use if you want to build this team-like setting on your account. That being said, if you do so you should make sure that you have a fixed schedule of who will use the account and when to avoid overwhelming your audience, repeating the same content twice, or creating a disconnect between what they are reading and seeing.

Get Involved in the Conversation

Twitter is all about conversation. If you want to market your business, you need to learn to do so in a way that gets you involved in the conversation. The best way to do this is to go to the main Twitter feed and begin looking at trending topics. Then, you can see which ones are relevant to the general public, as well as which ones are relevant to your unique industry. Once you have, you can read over the conversations and find ways to include yourself. General inclusion, as well as including yourself in a way that allows you to market your products or services are both great ways to get involved.

When conversing with others, you can use two different ways to do so: the first one is to comment on their post. This is a simple comment that is made under their post and that is viewable by all. Or, you can Retweet. Retweeting is like sharing their post and allows you to include a few words about how you feel about what has been said. Either way is a great method for getting involved and sharing in the conversation.

Post Relevant Content

Not everything on your page should be filled with Retweets and live conversation between you and other users. You are going to want to post organic, authentic content at least a few times per day on your page. Doing so means that you need to create your own post and share it with your audience. You can do so by tapping "Tweet" and writing a status update or sharing a picture, video, or link with your audience. Ideally, you should mix up what exactly you are sharing on a daily basis to avoid being seen as bland or repetitive in both what you are saying and the way you are saying it.

Your posts should be relevant, interesting, and entertaining in some form or another. Educating your audience, sharing something that will make them laugh or feel inspired, or simply showing off a new product in use is a great way to share. As mentioned in chapter 13, however, this is where many businesses can run into problems. Overly promoting yourself, sharing too many sales pitches, or trying to make hard sales on Twitter through this method will actually take away from your viewers' experience and thus minimize your exposure. People will not like or Retweet your content, meaning it will not be seen. If you want maximum exposure you should focus on keeping 80% of your weekly content engaging, interesting, entertaining, inspiring, or otherwise non-marketing related. The other 20% can be focused on marketing, but should always be done in a suggestive or polite way and not in a hard sales pitch way. In other words "What a heat wave! We have great products to protect your skin during the summer heat – check them out!" or "OMG I love the smell of our new sunscreen – pineapple is BLISS!" is effective, but "Sunscreen on sale for $13.99!" is not.

Chapter 15:
Paid Twitter Marketing

Using Twitter for paid marketing is a great way to get your account seen by a greater audience. Twitter has a great analytics software that makes discovering your demographic and marketing to them extremely simple. In 2019, marketing through paid Twitter advertisements will be a great way to get your name out there and get seen by the 47% of people who want to click your link and check out what you have to offer.

Twitter Analytics

The first step in creating your paid marketing campaign will be to look at your analytics and discover who is actually engaging with your profile. Twitter has in-depth analytics that shows you what age range, location, gender, and interests are all relevant to your ideal audience. Before you set your paid advertisement up, go check out your analytics and jot down this information to ensure that you know exactly who to target your ad toward when you are making it. Since these people are already actively engaging with you in a powerful way, you know that they will be most receptive of your paid campaign, making it even more effective than if you were to attempt to target a demographic that was not overly interested in what you were selling or sharing.

Set Your Objective

Every advertisement needs to have an objective. Your objective is simply to determine what you want to come of the advertisement. In 2019, it is projected that the best objectives will be to increase engagement and exposure and to encourage people to visit your website. Trying to sell specific products will not be as effective as simply trying to get people over to your website and then creating a funnel that drives them to your sales page or shop page so that they can purchase from you.

Pick Your Audience

With the information in-hand from your analytics, setting your audience for your advertisement will be easy. Here, you will use Twitter's targeting page to let Twitter know who you want to target the advertisement toward. You can determine what age and gender they are, what location they are from, and other information such as what they are interested in or what notable accounts they follow. These features allow you to set the parameter of who your demographic is, helping Twitter ensure that they market to the right people. Because Twitter has such an advanced analytics feature built-in, this should be extremely easy. Simply outline the exact audience as shown in your analytics and you are good to go!

Paying for Your Ad

Twitter uses a bidding style for their advertisements. This means that you bid on how much you want to spend on each engagement. You can set this custom by inputting what you are willing to spend, or you can set it to "automatic." Then, you can determine how much you want to spend overall. This will be your budget. So, your budget is how much you will spend overall, whereas your bid is how much you are willing to spend per engagement. Once you have more analytic results from previous ads, setting your bid per engagement can be done custom. Otherwise, it is easier to leave it to automatic so that you get the best chance of being placed in the best areas around the platform for viewership.

Create Your Ad

Lastly, you need to create the advertisement itself. When you are creating Tweets for your campaigns, you want to avoid using ones with mentions or hashtags, as these can actually draw people away from your campaign. Instead, use ones that are status updates, images, or videos complete with a call to actions that encourage your audience to sign up, visit your shop, or otherwise engage with you. These types of Tweets are far more direct and give your viewer a clear explanation on where to go and what to do. Because of that, you will get better results from your ad.

Twitter will use Tweets that you have already made in the past, allowing you to essentially boost 4 or 5 of them so they can be seen by others on Twitter who have not organically seen them. That being said, you want to create the Tweets in your timeline first using the advice from chapter 14 before creating your ad as these will become the Tweets for your campaign.

Once you have determined what Tweets to use, all that is left to do is hit "Launch." Then, you will review and confirm your campaign. Once you have, Twitter will ensure that it meets their standards before approving it within 24 hours. Then, you will be able to see your ad live on your page for whatever amount of time you have set within the parameters of your campaign.

Conclusion

Thank you for reading *Social Media Marketing 2019!*

I hope that this book was able to highlight the importance of the four major and primary social media platforms for you. Facebook, Instagram, YouTube, and Twitter are all actively working toward creating a strong social media experience for their users, including peer-to-peer and business-to-customer experiences. By understanding how these platforms will continue to grow in 2019 and what this means for your business, you can create a strong social media strategy for 2019 that will help launch you further into success.

If you are a new business going into 2019, these strategies will support you in starting out strong and making the most of these platforms. Now is a great time to get started as marketing online is being understood in a greater way and analytic tools on various platforms are stronger than ever before. If you have been in business for a while but are eager to get a great start into 2019, these strategies will support you in really giving it your all and maximizing your online success in 2019.

Remember, the marketing theme for 2019 is *social*. Maximizing your social impact by engaging more, sharing more, and showing more is the best way to interact with your customers. If you are not already, the next step for you in your strategy is to begin taking advantage of these many new social sharing features to create stronger connections with your audience. This will keep you relevant, interesting, and engaging going into 2019.

Lastly, if you enjoyed this book *Social Media Marketing* I ask that you please take the time to leave a review on Amazon. Your feedback would be greatly appreciated.

Thank you!